Wild Weather

REVISED AND UPDATED

Catherine Chambers

www.heinemann.co.uk/library

Visit our website to find out more information about **Heinemann Library** books.

To order:
- ☎ Phone ++44 (0)1865 888112
- 🖷 Send a fax to ++44 (0)1865 314091
- 🖥 Visit the Heinemann Bookshop at www.heinemann.co.uk/library to browse our catalogue and order online.

First published in Great Britain by Heinemann Library, Halley Court, Jordan Hill, Oxford OX2 8EJ, part of Harcourt Education. Heinemann is a registered trademark of Harcourt Education.

Editorial: Clare Lewis
Designed: Steve Mead and Q2A
Illustrations: Paul Bale
Picture Research: Tracy Cummins
Production: Julie Carter

Originated by Modern Age Repro
Printed and bound in China by South China Printing Company Limited

10 digit ISBN 0 431 15088 5
13 digit ISBN 978 0 431 15088 8

11 10 09 08 07
10 9 8 7 6 5 4 3 2 1

British Library Cataloguing in Publication Data

Chambers, Catherine
Wild Weather: Tornado. – 2nd Edition – Juvenile literature
551.5'53
A full catalogue record for this book is available from the British Library.

Acknowledgements
The Publishers would like to thank the following for permission to reproduce photographs: AP Photo/The Advocate Messenger/Clay Jackson, p28, Associated Press pp 14, 20, 23, 27, China Photos/Getty Images p8, Corbis pp21, 25, FLPA p22, Oxford Scientific Films pp4, 11, 15, PA Photos p26, Photodisc p16, Jim Reed/Corbis p19, Rex Features p12, Robert Harding Picture Library p5, Michael Rolands/istockphoto p29, Science Photo Library pp10, 13, 18, Stone pp7, 9, 17, 24.

Cover photograph of a tornado in Kansas, USA, reproduced with permission of Erik Nguyen/Jim Reed Photography/Corbis.

The Publishers would like to thank Mark Rogers and the Met Office for their assistance with the preparation of this book.

Every effort has been made to contact copyright holders of any material reproduced in this book.
Any omissions will be rectified in subsequent printings if notice is given to the Publisher.

The paper used to print this book comes from sustainable resources.

Any words appearing in the text in bold, **like this**, are explained in the Glossary.

Contents

What is a tornado?

A tornado is a moving, spinning **funnel** of wind. It swirls from a dark, towering cloud. The wind in a tornado is very strong. The tornado can suck up anything in its path.

■ *Tornadoes are made from dark storm clouds.*

■ *Tornadoes can cause a lot of damage.*

The spinning wind throws everything out at the sides as it moves along. This makes a huge cloud of dust and **debris** around the tornado.

Where do tornadoes happen?

Tornadoes can happen in most places. This map shows some parts of the world where tornadoes happen. There are many tornadoes in the United States.

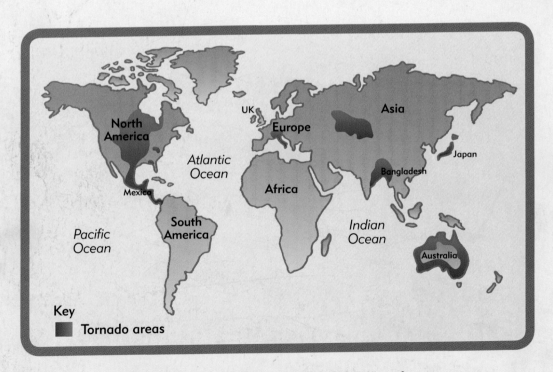

■ *The areas shown in organge are the places where tornadoes often happen.*

■ *This farm is in Tornado Alley in the United States.*

This part of the United States lies in an area called Tornado Alley. It has more tornadoes than anywhere else in the world.

Wind and cloud

Wind is made when **masses** of air move around. Some masses are cold. Others are warm. Warm air usually rises. Cold air rushes in to fill the space it leaves. This causes strong winds.

■ *In strong winds, umbrellas can be turned inside out!*

■ *This picture of clouds was taken from space.*

Water vapour is always in the air. When air rises it cools. The vapour turns into droplets of water.

Why do tornadoes happen?

Tornadoes form in storm clouds. They happen in hot, moist weather. Heavy storm clouds form. Clouds suck up warm, moist air from below. Cool air blows across the top of the cloud. These movements make a twisting wind.

■ *Storm clouds often form in warm weather.*

■ *A waterspout is a tornado over water.*

The spinning wind makes a cone shaped
funnel that can dip right down to the ground.
Sometimes tornadoes move over water. This
makes a **waterspout**.

What are tornadoes like?

People can see most tornadoes coming. They can also see dust and **debris** swirling around the bottom of the **funnel**. Yet no one knows exactly where the tornado will go.

■ *Even if you see a tornado it is hard to tell exactly where it will go.*

■ *Clouds that form tornadoes can also make lightning.*

Tornadoes often happen as part of thunderstorms. People see lightning and hear thunder. Heavy rain falls.

Harmful tornadoes

The winds in tornadoes travel faster than any other winds. Tornadoes only affect a narrow area. They destroy anything in their path.

■ *Some houses can be destroyed by tornadoes while houses next to them are untouched.*

hailstones

■ *Hailstones can add to the damage caused by tornadoes.*

Dark tornado clouds can hold **masses** of icy **hailstones**. The hailstones fall and sometimes hurt people and animals. They can also damage buildings and **crops**.

Tornado Alley

Oklahoma is in the middle of the United States. It is part of Tornado Alley. A lot of damaging tornadoes happen here.

North America

Atlantic Ocean

Pacific Ocean

• Oklahoma City

■ *Winds can sweep across the flat **plains** around Oklahoma.*

■ *Tornadoes like this one can destroy buildings.*

Terrible tornadoes hit Oklahoma on 3 May 1999. They sucked up and threw out everything in their paths. The flying **debris** hit people and buildings – 45 people were killed.

Preparing for a tornado

Weather forecasters tell **emergency services** when a tornado has formed. The emergency services use radio, television, and the Internet to warn people about the tornado.

■ *Weather forecasters use computers to help them work out where a tornado will travel next.*

■ *It is exciting to chase tornadoes. It can also be dangerous.*

Storm-chasers are people who try to get close to tornadoes. The storm-chasers take pictures of the tornadoes. They also warn weather forecasters that a tornado is coming.

Tornado warning

On 3 April 1974 **weather forecasters** in the
United States knew that many tornadoes
were coming. They sent out over 160 tornado
warnings to 14 **states**.

■ *Weather warnings
can help give people
time to prepare for
a tornado.*

■ *The 1974 tornadoes were some of the worst in history.*

On that day, 148 tornadoes struck. Over 300 people were killed and over 30,000 buildings were destroyed. No one could stop the tornadoes.

Coping with tornadoes

Tornadoes can damage all types of buildings. In some places, people are able to go to specially built tornado-safe shelters when they know a tornado is coming.

■ *Tornado shelters are often underground.*

■ *These cars have been thrown about by a tornado.*

People do not stay in their cars when a tornado strikes. Tornadoes are so powerful that they can pick up cars and throw them high into the air.

Tornadoes and nature

There are many stories of frogs falling from the sky. This is because they can get sucked up by tornadoes and then fall to the ground again when the tornado is over.

■ *Tornadoes over water may pick up frogs or fish.*

■ *Tornadoes can flatten crops.*

Tornadoes often blow across fields where **crops** are grown. They destroy the crops that lie in their path. A tornado's path can be over 100 metres (300 feet) wide.

To the rescue!

After a tornado, rescuers often find people trapped underneath flattened buildings. Ambulances take **injured** people to hospital.

■ *People can be injured by tornadoes.*

Emergency tornado shelters can protect people from tornadoes. The people's homes may still be destroyed by the tornado.

Adapting to tornadoes

People in the United States learn how to shelter from tornadoes. Here, some children are learning what to do during a tornado drill at school.

■ *People who live in tornado areas must be prepared.*

■ *A siren tells people to prepare for a tornado.*

Areas that have a lot of tornados often have sirens. The sirens make a loud noise when tornados are nearby. People rush to get inside a tornado shelter or a strong building.

Fact file

◆ The worst tornado that we know about happened in Bangladesh on 2 April 1977. Around 900 people died.

◆ Tornadoes can spin at up to 480 kilometres per hour (300 miles per hour). They can travel over 350 kilometres (217 miles). Tornadoes can reach 1,000 metres (3300 feet) into the sky.

◆ Scientists use invisible **radio signals** to find out if a tornado is forming. The signals bounce off **ice crystals** in the dark cloud. The signals make a pattern. If the pattern makes a hook shape, a tornado is forming.

Glossary

crops plants grown for food

debris earth and broken objects that are thrown around by the tornado

emergency services people who help us when there is a disaster. The police, ambulance, and fire services are all emergency services.

funnel long, thin tube

hailstones hard balls of ice that come from thunderclouds

ice crystals tiny pieces of frozen water

injured hurt

masses huge areas or amounts of something

plain large area of flat land

radio signals waves of sound that travel through the air

states areas of the USA that make some of their own laws. California and Florida are states.

waterspout huge funnel of water made when a tornado whirls over a lake, wide river, or the sea

water vapour water that has changed into a gas

weather forecasters scientists who work out what the weather will be like in the future

More books to read

Weather Watch: *Wind*, Honor Head (QED, 2006).

The Weather: *Wind*, Angela Royston (Chrysalis Children's Books, 2004).

Index

Titles in the *Wild Weather* series include:

Hardback 978-0-431-15081-9

Hardback 978-0-431-15082-6

Hardback 978-0-431-15083-3

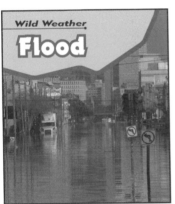

Hardback 978-0-431-15080-2

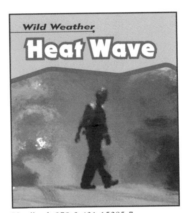

Hardback 978-0-431-15085-7

Hardback 978-0-431-15086-4

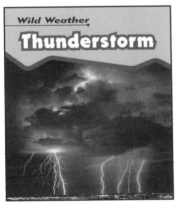

Hardback 978-0-431-15087-1

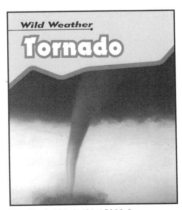

Hardback 978-0-431-15088-8

Find out about other titles Heinemann Library on our website www.heinemann.co.uk/library